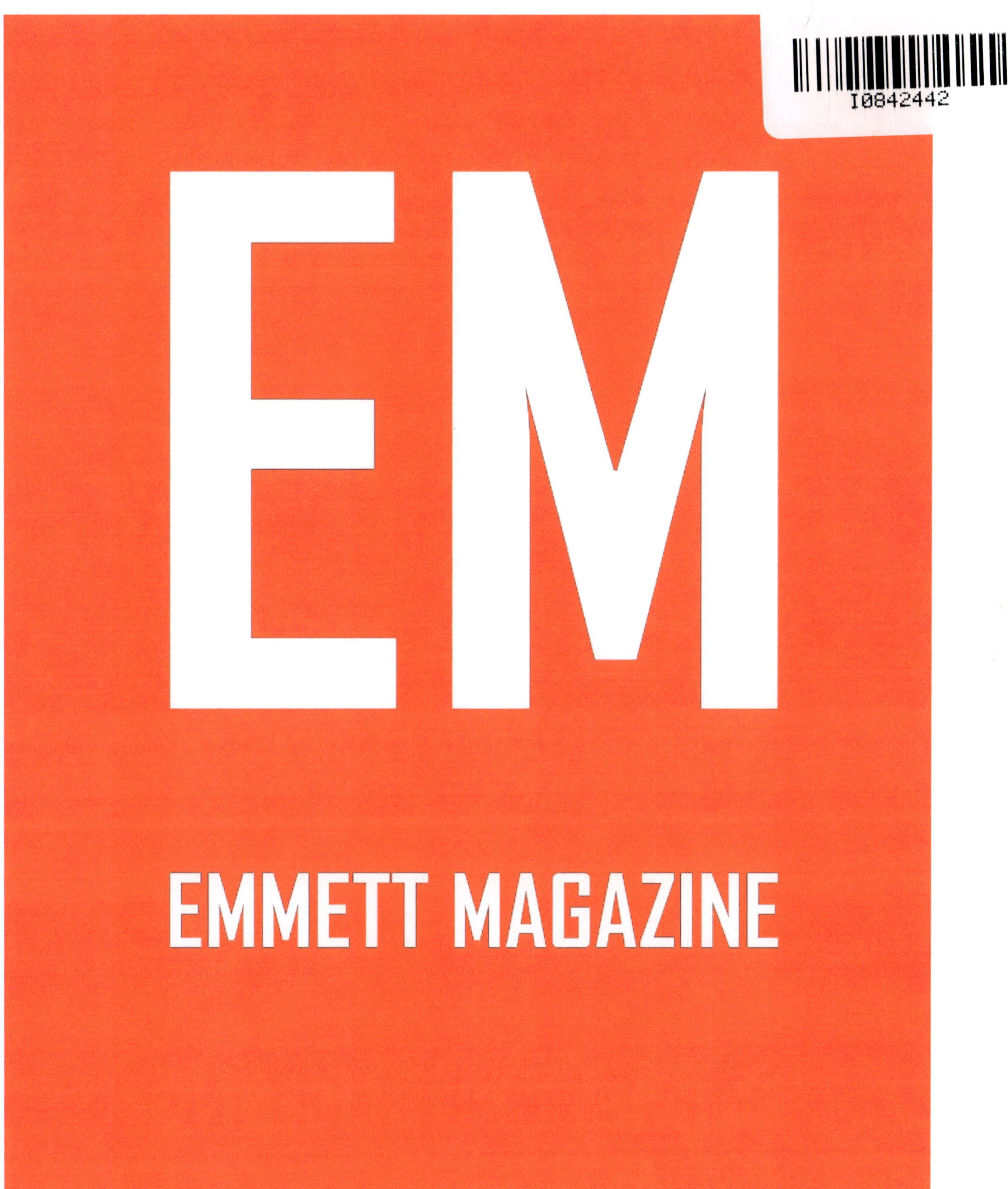
EM
EMMETT MAGAZINE

TABLE OF CONTENTS

THE KATHY HARRELSON STORY

Pages

3-13

STAGE & SCREEN

ACTRESS HARRIET BURNETTE

Pages

14-31

EMMETT PUBLISHING

The Kathy Harrelson Story

By Emmett Williams, Jr.

Katherine Harrelson (Kathy) is originally from the small town of Milton, North Carolina in Caswell County where gardening is a tradition.

As a youth, she was inspired by her Mother and Grandmother. Her Mother, Penolia Coleman-Lea a very caring and patient person who believed in life-long learning. Grandma Rosa Lea believed in the Mentoring and the Village concept. The 4-H Club helped to shape her destiny and encouraged community service.

Inspiring Figures and Mentors of Kathy's: the late Shirley Chisolm, the late Brenda Bruner, the late Rev. Dr. Mazie Butler Ferguson and Meg Sternberg. The Women who she cited as helping her achieve her goals were: Delores Crockett, Congresswoman Alma Adams, Juanita Bryant, Thealeeta Monet, Dianne Stanley, Joyce Gioia and Marilyn Rankin.

What inspired you originally? Was it a person or a need to solve a problem?

Growing up in a small town and going to a segregated school where the use of second hand books was the norm and the Library being many miles away, it was a dream of mine to ensure that every child, no matter where they lived, would have access to the resources and experiences that inner city children have. That was my motivation and inspiration to develop wraparound services and educational experiences beneficial to becoming well rounded citizens.

The stereotypes were quite obvious to me growing up including all of the isms. Therefore, I felt the Divine Master positioned me to learn and to teach in such a way that every child would be able to grow and learn to advocate for themselves. Additionally, Economic Development is a family issue therefore, I felt it imperative that youth learn Financial Literacy, Community Engagement, Economic self-sufficiency, and Democracy, just to name a few.

Do you have any statistics you can share as a result of the programs you created or support?

5,486 young women graduated from the program. 92% received college degrees, 14% hold advanced degrees and 4% hold certifications. We now can claim Social Workers, Psychologists, Lawyers, Administrators, Accountants, Bankers, Fashion Designers, Teachers, Medical Professionals and many Entrepreneurs.

Would you name some of the other local business, teachers, politicians, churches who have been involved in your collective efforts?

Kathy Knight, an avid volunteer, Perry Graves, Transportation Coordination, Alba Mendoza Allen, first Fitness Instructor, Cynthia Henderson, Philanthropist, Dr. Comfort (Professor @ High Point University, Dr. Nido Quebin, President of High Point University, Dr. Gloria Scott, Past President of Bennett College, Senator Gladys Robinson, Attorney Henri Norris, Gloria Sexton and April Reese, Former Public Relations Director, NC Council for Women.

How can parents help?

Parents can help by volunteering, serving on the Parent Advisory Board and participating in planning fundraisers. Additionally, it is imperative as we fight for democracy at a critical time in our lives that parents participate in advocacy training.

The Women's Foundation of North Carolina, Inc.

Is an alliance of women, working together.

To:

- **Promote philanthropy for women and children**
- **Improve economic vitality for women and children**
- **Develop and expand leadership capacities for women and children**
- **And, fund programs that enable women and children to maximize their full potential.**

An affiliate program of the Women's Foundation of North Carolina

HISTORY:

Leadership C.O.N.N.E.C.T.I.O.N.S., was established in 1991, with a grant from the Women's Bureau, US Department of Labor. The program's Founder, Katherine Harrelson affectionately known to participants as (Ms. Kathy), worked as a volunteer director for 33 years and continues to work in the same capacity. Multiple funding sources were acknowledged during the journey. They were: the Z. Smith Reynolds Foundation, the Governor's Crime Commission, The Old North State Medical Society and Foundation.

During the 15th year of Leadership C.O.N.N.E.C.T.I.O.N.S, participants in college or college graduates took on the role of program staff. The program, during its inception was designed as a Peer to Peer training program, utilizing a three-tier mentoring process. Peer, Career and Social. The program grew each year becoming one of the most diverse sought after girls program in North Carolina in 2006 nationally. In 1999, Training Magazine wrote an article about the program entitled: "Mentoring for Tomorrow's Workplace" We were told that the magazine was distributed to 5,000 corporations across the United States. The model consists of Awards named for Career women who had made significant contributions to history. After each girl reached the milestone criteria, the women would come to the gala and surprise them with their awards. The following awards became very popular and motivated young women to succeed. **The Alma Adams Cultural Ambassador Award**, the **Katie Dorsett Academic Excellence Award** named after the late **Dr. Katie Dorsett, The Juanita Bryant Leadership Award, The Claudette Burroughs-White Young Juvenile Award,** named after the Late **Claudette Burroughs-White, The Thealeeta Monet, Health and Wellness Award, The Velma Speight-Buford Education Excellence Award, the Yvonne Johnson, Public Service Award** and the **Marikay Abuzuaiter Community Service Award.**

Prior to the closing of **a Girl's Youth Development Cente**r sponsored by **the NC Juvenile Justice System**. Under the then very capable leadership of Judy Julian, our college students were asked to write a curriculum for "troubled girls". Seven students wrote a curriculum entitled **"Stand Tall & Reach" (S.T.A.R.)** this became the first Peer taught program for a girls YDC, so popular that requests were coming from other YDC's in the United States. After that eleven-month experience, the late **Doris Mack/Judy Julian Resource Center for Girls** opened.

Several projects have evolved based on Alumnae members' upskilling and recognizing that creative opportunities teach life skills that are difficult to teach in academic settings due to learning style differences. Therefore, connecting colors were born. **Young Women in Pink** (a philanthropy leadership skills building opportunity that enhances math skills) became a youth fundraising opportunity thereby affording an opportunity for the girls to provide funding to breast cancer organizations. That was followed by **Young Women in Purple** (violence prevention). **YWIP, Young Women in Gold** (Education), etc.

"Democracy without Walls" became one of the most popular program opportunities after Civics Education was not available in some of the school settings. That was followed by another popular project entitled **"Economic Wisdom for the Next Generation"** and **STEM** education. Covid 19 prohibited college experiences and annual fundraisers. Therefore the creation of the

"Red Carpet Kids" health, fitness and wellness project was a way to keep participants engaged. Gifted participants sang with professionals like **Sister Sledge** and sang ahead of a **Harold Melvin and his Blue Notes**.

In July of 2023, LC was tapped to develop a co-ed empowerment program for the **"Michelle Obama Empowerment Academy"** that starts each school day with a fitness opportunity for kids that encourages healthy eating through musical performances, dance and -3-other artistic fitness opportunities at middle and elementary schools. Students have an opportunity to write their own poetic version of why healthy eating and exercise are important. The youth are so excited to know that they are participating in the **"Healthy Hunger Free Kids"** project. 132 girls and boys were able to participate in the opportunity from September 2023 through May, 2024. The project is facilitated by **Ty Gibson** known to youth as "TyG".

Gloria Bass, the Youth Community Advocate and **Trades Trainer**, focused on ensuring children with learning style differences were supported with specialized training, tutoring and other academic support to ensure they are not only nutritionally and physically fit but are able to matriculate to the next academic level. An Architect by academic training, uses her brick making skills to teach youth to build brick enhancing their mathematical skills.

PHOTO BY TIM PIERCE

Stan Montgomery, Deputy Administrator for Special Services, spearheads the Community Junior Cadet Program that is designed to build on the strengths of participants' informal entrepreneurial skills by redirecting the negative into positive community building by training them to recognize and report crime to law enforcement. They will be upskilled to program robots in their community to sniff out crime by developing positive skills that will provide them an opportunity to positively assist in preventing community crime.

Red Carpet Kids

Sister Sledge

The Singers performed at a fund-raising event to benefit the Children, who were invited to remain on stage and perform with the group.

Community Junior Cadets

Congresswoman Alma Adams.

THE WOMEN'S FOUNDATION OF NORTH CAROLINA

www.womensfoundationofnc.com

Visit the site listed above to learn more.

Donations welcome.

CONTACT

info@womensfoundationofnc.com

Stage & Screen

ACTRESS HARRIET BURNETTE

By Emmett A. Williams, Jr.

THE INTERVIEW

EM

Good morning Harriet,

How are you doing this morning?

Harriet Burnette

Doing absolutely amazing!

EM

Awesome.

Harriet, please introduce yourself to the audience and tell them where you're originally from.

Harriet Burnette

I am from a small town called Whitakers, NC.

EM

Great, and when did you know you wanted to have a career in the arts as an Actress?

Harriet Burnette

Wow. I guess I actually realized that at a young age, but realistically 11 years ago was when I actually started really getting serious in the business and that's where it all started about 11 years ago, I was introduced to acting.

EM

Okay, so quick question before then, did you study Acting?

Harriet Burnette

I had one acting class I guess coarser when really just an acting class and that was years ago before I even really-really got deep into acting but most of my acting was done by roles like that was about referrals and

Casting Calls.

EM

What types of characters interest you?

Harriet Burnette

I guess most of my roles have been like the motherly Auntie type but I love being versatile I've done the Boujie, know-it-all characters, I've enjoyed doing caring characters, people like that my mother. All of those characters had really-really opened a lot of doors for me but I want to play many more types than those.

EM

OK, is there any actor or actress's performance that inspired you originally?

Harriet Burnette

I've always loved love-loved Angela Bassett because she's has the diversity that I like and she's very classy and sophisticated. I like that about her as well. She's very true to her craft as I've watched her in over the years. So Angela Bassett has really been the one that I really got me into wanting to be an actress.

EM

Now, your current project can you talk about that, and the role you play?

Harriet Burnette

"Jessica's Drama"

That is a very, very dear project to my heart, I get to play the lead role, all business, very classy, sophisticated, successful meddles in everybody's business, but like to get things done and thinks that she's the one that can handle it and everything. It's touching, family oriented experience that I think that everybody can relate to.

Mrs. Donna D. Walker is the Director of that particular film and I'm very excited about that. We're still in the process of finishing it. So that role is very dear to me. That's one of the most recent ones that I've got going on at this point with others on the on the back burner right now. Donna is also the Writer.

EM

Awesome, Writer and Director.

EM

Who's the Producer?

Harriet Burnette

I believe she and her husband, Wayne Walker produced.

EM

How many roles have you played altogether?

Harriet Burnette

I've been in over 30 roles, some are on Amazon, Tubi and YouTube at this time.

EM

All right. How did you find out about this opportunity? Was it a casting call or referral or an agent? Do you have an agent you want to name?

Harriet Burnette

Actually I do not have an agent. Most of my stuff has been done by referrals, and that's basically how I got the Lead Role in Jessica's Drama, and was asked to star.

"I'm Jessica and I bring the Drama."

EM

Okay. Do you have previous work on YouTube because I could mention them?

Harriet Burnette

Yes, I have a couple films on YouTube. One film is Chains2Break by Earlina Gilford Shine. Another film is, The More Things Change by Randy Wrenn.

EM

Other than film, have you done Theatre/Plays?

Harriet Burnette

Yes, I have done several plays. Dem Chuuurch Mothers by Jojo Gardner, Bruised But Not Broken & Motherless Child By Eric Swindell, I Too Survived by Angelyric Productions & The Portrayal of God's Anointed, by Betty Humphrey Breeden, Actress and Best vocalist.

EM

Okay, cool. What other skills do you have?

So you sing, Harriet?

Harriet Burnette

Yes, I have been singing all my life.

EM

Did you train for it or are you just a natural?

Harriet Burnette

I did go to Winston-Salem State for about a year, and I was a music major there. But most of my singing was natural.

EM

Do you sing in a church?

Harriet Burnette

I do. Same church I used to sing in the band years ago, I do events as well.

EM

Anything else you want to add?

Harriet Burnette

Yes, I've been a model for over 44 years. As CEO of Del Carlos Productions LLC, I teach kids and adults modeling through workshops and one on one classes. At present I am spokesperson for The Peace Is Priceless Brand by CEO Acy Brown. In house model for designer Ciata Kromah of JaCha Trends African Clothing.

As for my singing, I started singing a very young age in church and now I also sing in my plays and movies. My singing skills come naturally from my Mother. Although I did go to school at WSSU as a music major for a little while before moving to Washington DC.

EM

Awesome. Okay, I think we got enough to start, and we'll just finish it up later on. I will check the quality of all of this. Plus, regardless, it will be in the magazine for sure.

I might use an audio file for our channel if it's good enough, I'll spin it into more promos later on.

EM

Could you say your name for an audio clip for our **EMMETT-TV** YouTube channel?

Harriet Burnette

Like now? Like, right now?

EM

Yes.

Harriet Burnette

"I'm Harriet Burnette, the actress. You can see me on **EMMETT-TV."**

EM

Thanks for speaking with EM.

Harriet Burnette

Thank you. Bye-bye.

Harriet Burnette and her Mother.

Top Left is me as Aunt Penny in 17 Days, Top Right, Grandma Wells in Chains2Break writer Earlina Gilford Shine, Center Left as Jessica in Jessica's Drama, Writer Donna Walker, Center Right as Dean Wormer in The More Things Change. Bottom Left as Jessica. Bottom Right is Fashion by Ciata Kromah, Liberia.

A.C.E. AWARDS

THE
AWARDS
ARTISTS CELEBRATING EXCELLENCE.

THE
CE
AWARDS

THE
CE
AWARDS

THE

CE
AW

AWARDS
ARTISTS CELEBRATING EXCELLENCE.

ARTISTS C

" TAKE
THE
CE
WWW.TH

Jessica's Drama Actress Burnette and Writer/Co-Director Walker.

DONNA D. WALKER WRITER/DIRECTOR

"Jessica's Drama"

EM
EMMETT MAGAZINE